weblinks

You don't need a computer to use this book. But, for readers who do have access to the Internet, the book provides links to recommended websites which offer additional information and resources on the subject.

You will find weblinks boxes like this on some pages of the book.

> **weblinks**
>
> For more information about coastlines, go to www.waylinks.co.uk/GeogDetective/Coastlines

waylinks.co.uk

To help you find the recommended websites easily and quickly, weblinks are provided on our own website, **waylinks.co.uk.** These take you straight to the relevant websites and save you typing in the Internet address yourself.

Internet safety

- Never give out personal details, which include: your name, address, school, telephone number, email address, password and mobile number.
- Do not respond to messages which make you feel uncomfortable – tell an adult.
- Do not arrange to meet in person someone you have met on the Internet.
- Never send your picture or anything else to an online friend without a parent's or teacher's permission.
- If you see anything that worries you, tell an adult.

A note to adults
Internet use by children should be supervised. We recommend that you install filtering software which blocks unsuitable material.

Website content

The weblinks for this book are checked and updated regularly. However, because of the nature of the Internet, the content of a website may change at any time, or a website may close down without notice. While the Publishers regret any inconvenience this may cause readers, they cannot be responsible for the content of any website other than their own.

WAYLAND

Coastlines

Jen Green

WAYLAND

First published in 2007 by Wayland

Editor: Hayley Fairhead
Designer: Simon Morse
Maps and artwork: Peter Bull
Cartoon artwork: Richard Hook

Wayland
338 Euston Road
London NW1 3BH

Wayland
Level 17/207 Kent Street
Sydney, NSW 2000

Green, Jen
Coastlines. - (The geography detective investigates)
1. Coasts - Juvenile literature
I. Title
551.4'57

ISBN 978-0-7502-5049-8

Printed in China

Wayland is a division of Hachette Children's Books.

Picture acknowledgements: Christophe Boisvieux/Corbis: 1,9b, Chinch Gryniewicz/Ecoscene/Corbis: 4, Jon Hicks/Corbis: 5t, Sergio Pitamitz/Corbis: 5b, Craig Tuttle/Corbis; 6, Robert Holmes/Corbis: 7, P.J. Sharpe/zefa/Corbis: 9t, Clint Garnham/Alamy: 10, Robert Estall/Alamy: 11, Danny Lehman/Corbis: 12, Stuart Westmorland/ Corbis: 13, Remi Benali/Corbis: 14, fstop2/Alamy: 15, Kennan Ward/Corbis: 16, Sally Morgan/Ecoscene/Corbis: 17, Matthew Polak/Sygma/Corbis: 18, Lowell Georgia/Corbis: 19, Travel Ink/Alamy: 20, Bob Krist/Corbis: 21, Edward Bent/Ecoscene: 22, Reuters/Corbis: 23, Mike Theiss/Jim Reed Photography/Corbis: 24, Kimimasa Mayama/Reuters/Corbis: 25t, Yann Arthus-Bertrand/ Corbis: 25b, Joe Cornish/NTPL: 26, Stuart Westmorland/Corbis: 27, Richard Klune/Corbis: 28, Pierre Tostee/ZUMA/Corbis: 29.

Cover: People relax on a beach in Gorey, Jersey with Mont Orguell Castle in the distance.

Contents

Words that appear in **bold** can be found in the glossary on page 30.

Answers to Sherlock Bones' questions can be found on page 31.

SAFETY FIRST

Make sure you ask an adult to help you when you are working near water. Always take care when you are close to the water's edge.

What are coastlines?

Coastlines are found wherever the land meets the ocean. The world's seven continents all have long coastlines. Thousands of islands add to the total of over 500,000 km of coastline worldwide.

FOCUS ON

Long coastlines

The country with the longest coastline is Canada, with 244,800 km of coastline. Russia, Indonesia, Greenland, Australia, the USA, Japan and Norway also have very long coastlines. The coastline of England, Wales and Scotland is a total of 14,500 km long.

Wild coastal scenery at Caswell Bay, Gower, Wales.

The scenery on coastlines is very varied. Towering **cliffs**, sand and **shingle** beaches, **mudflats**, **saltmarshes** and river **estuaries** may be found along a stretch of coast. Palm trees, coral reefs and mangrove swamps may be found on coastlines in the **tropics**, while polar coasts are edged with sea ice. This varied scenery provides habitats for all kinds of wildlife, including fish, birds, seals, turtles, shellfish and crabs.

Tourism is the main industry on coasts such as the Coasta Blanca in Spain.

Coasts provide people with fish for food and access to the sea, so people can travel around by boat. Many coastlines have been settled since ancient times. Around the world, coastlines that were once wild have now been developed, with busy harbours and docks, or resorts with hotels.

Coastlines are places that are always changing. They change in shape as the sea **erodes** the land, or drops sand and pebbles to form beaches. People also change coastlines by building sea walls, quays and piers. Some of these changes harm coastal habitats and their wildlife by causing pollution. However, people are now learning to take better care of coastlines.

DETECTIVE WORK

Use a map of your country or local area to find out about the coastline nearest to you. How far away is it? If possible, visit your local coast. What kind of scenery can be found there – are there cliffs, beaches or wetlands? Is the coastline wild or developed? Where is the nearest big port?

Ice shelves extend out to sea, along the Antarctic coast.

What forces shape coastlines?

The pounding waves and the action of the tides are the main forces at work shaping coastlines. Waves form as winds blow across the surface of the sea. Out to sea the water **circulates** freely, producing low waves called **rollers**. In shallow water, waves hit the seabed and the water crashes up into the air.

Night and day, waves wear away the **shore**, in a process called **erosion**. The sheer weight of crashing water wears away the rock, while grit and pebbles carried by the waves act like sandpaper. Waves wear deep grooves into the base of **cliffs**. When the rock on top collapses, the cliff moves further inland.

In calm weather, waves slap gently at the shoreline. During storms they crash down with great force.

At low tide the sea retreats, exposing more of the shoreline.

What clues might you find on a beach to show how far the sea reaches at high tide?

Tidal ranges

The difference in water level between high and low tide is called the **tidal range**. The Bay of Fundy on Canada's east coast has the world's greatest tidal range, up to 16 m. The tidal range on British coasts is also quite high, at around 5 m.

Twice a day, the sea rises up the shore and then falls back again. This is called the tide. The movement of the sea during the tides causes erosion. Tides are mainly caused by the pull of the Moon's **gravity** on the oceans. As the Moon circles the Earth, it pulls the sea towards it, making the water pile up in a mound (see diagram). The amount of water on either side of the mound is reduced (low tide). As the Earth spins east, the mound travels across the oceans, surging onto coasts (high tides). The Sun also pulls the oceans. When the two pulls act together, a very high tide occurs.

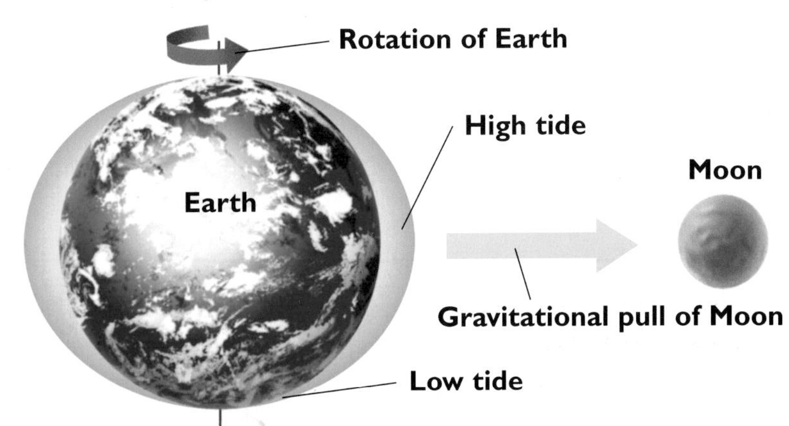

How are coastlines shaped by erosion?

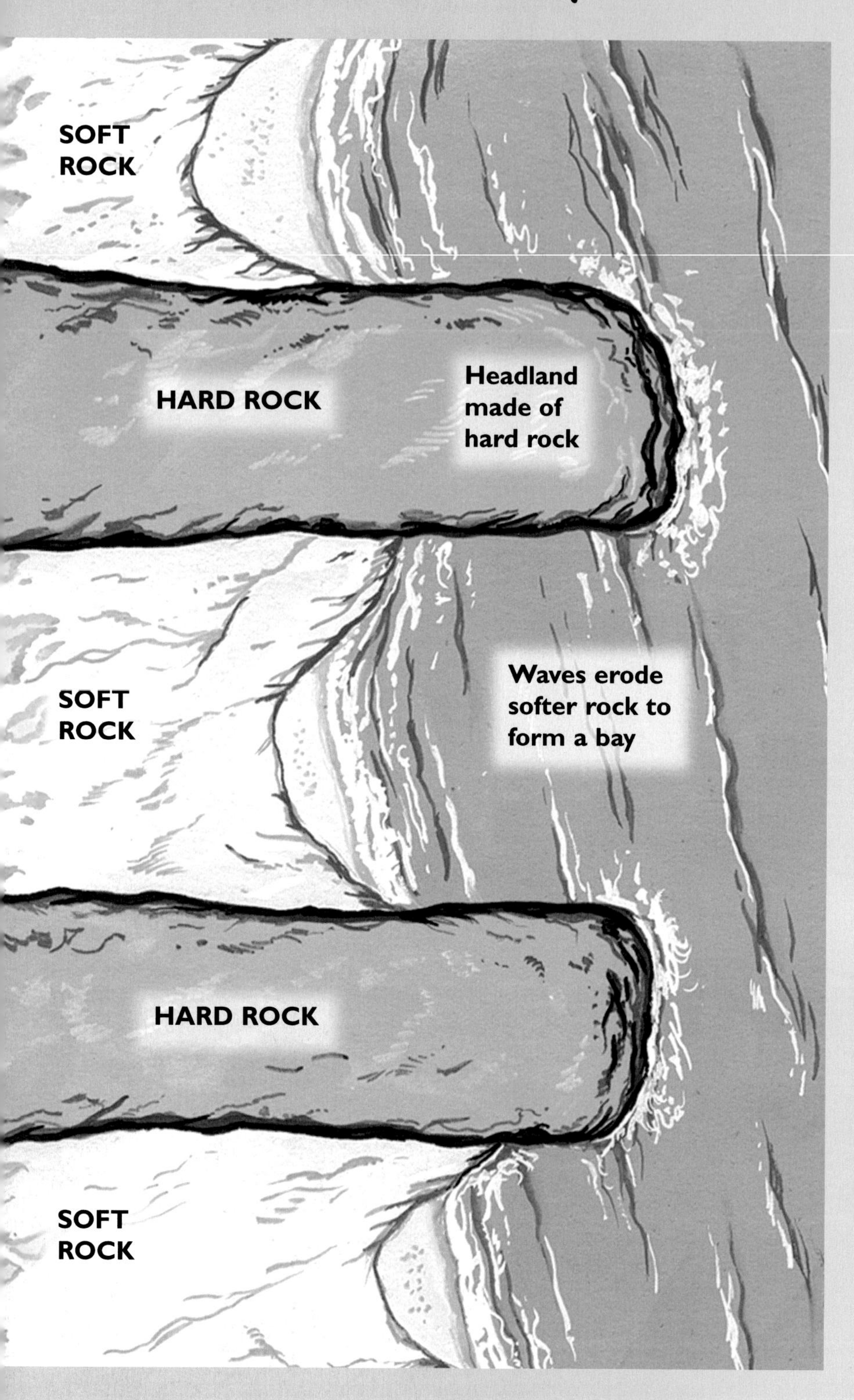

Headlands are formed as the sea wears away the soft rock.

The speed at which coasts are worn away partly depends on the type of rocks found there. The sea **erodes** the soft rocks, such as chalk, forming curving bays and coves (small bays). Hard rocks, such as granite, take a long time to wear away and so form **headlands** that extend out to sea.

Coves sometimes form when a band of rock runs along the coast, with soft rock, such as chalk, behind it. If the sea breaks through the hard rock, the soft rock behind erodes quickly. This can create an almost circular cove, such as Lulworth Cove in southern Britain.

Cliffs form where high ground meets the sea. The world's highest cliffs, on Hawaii, are 1 km tall. **Fjords** are bays with sheer cliffs that run deep inland. They are found in places such as Scotland, Alaska and Norway. Fjords were once U-shaped valleys by the sea that were carved by glaciers during **Ice Ages**. When the last Ice Age ended, the **climate** warmed and the ice melted. Sea levels rose to flood the valleys, which became fjords.

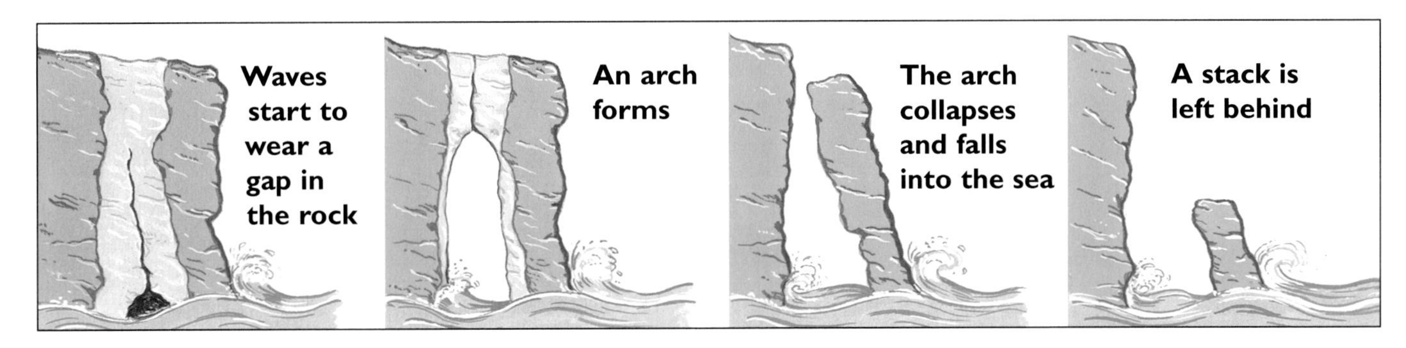

Arches and stacks are formed as the sea wears a gap into the rock.

Along some stretches of coast you will find caves, arches and rocky pillars called **stacks**. Caves form where the sea carves a hollow in the rock. An arch may appear where the sea cuts into a headland, which eventually wears right through. As **erosion** continues, the arch collapses to form a stack.

This spectacular arch on Britain's south coast is called Durdle Door.

Steep cliffs surround this fjord in Norway.

How do beaches, spits and bars form?

Along many coastlines, the sea is eroding the land, but in some places, the opposite is happening. New land is appearing, as beaches, **spits** and islands are created by the sea.

Beaches are strips of coastline covered with mud and rocky fragments, such as sand, **shingle** or pebbles. These loose materials are either carried by rivers from inland out to sea, or they are pieces of rock worn from **cliffs** and headlands, and smashed to pieces by the waves.

Rocks and shingle from this bay are being dragged further along the coast by the waves.

Where waves strike the **shore** at an angle, rocks and shingle may be dragged along the coast. This process is called **longshore drift**. Waves just out to sea may also shift debris sideways. Sooner or later, the waves reach a sheltered area. They slow down and drop their load. Beaches form where rocky fragments wash ashore, usually in sheltered bays and coves.

Spits are long fingers of land attached to the shore, made of sand, mud or pebbles. They form where waves drop rocky material in the shelter of a **headland** or a river mouth. A spit stretching right across a bay is called a **bar**. Sometimes sand or stones pile up out to sea to form a **barrier island**. The coast of eastern USA has many spits and barrier islands running along the shore.

Chesil Beach

Chesil Beach off the coastline of southern Britain is the longest bar in Europe, at 16 km long. Along this bar the sea has dropped pebbles according to size. Potato-sized pebbles are found at one end, with pea-sized pebbles at the other. Waves drop large pebbles first, carrying small ones further along the bar.

A spit at the mouth of the River Alde in Suffolk. The mouth of the river is visible in the distance.

DETECTIVE WORK

Take a trip to your nearest beach. Identify the type of beach – is it sandy, pebbly or shingly? Can you identify the type of rock, and can you see where the rocks might have come from by looking at nearby cliffs?

How do islands and coral reefs form?

Islands lie off many coasts. Being surrounded by water, they have their own long coastlines. There are two main types of islands: continental islands and oceanic islands. The two are formed in different ways.

The islands of Hawaii in the Pacific are a chain of volcanoes.

Oceanic islands often lie far out to sea. Many are the tops of undersea volcanoes. **Lava** erupts from under the sea and piles up, eventually rising above the water to make a volcanic island. The islands of Hawaii in the Pacific and the Lesser Antilles in the Caribbean formed in this way.

FOCUS ON

Record breaking islands

Greenland is the world's largest island, covering 2,175,600 sq km. The second-largest is New Guinea covering 777,000 sq km, followed by Borneo, Madagascar, Baffin Island and Sumatra. Australia's Great Barrier Reef is the world's longest coral reef, at approximately 2,000 km long.

Continental islands are found in the shallow waters off the world's continents. They are partly formed and shaped by changing sea levels. Many, including the British Isles, were once part of nearby mainlands. Britain was cut off from Europe when sea levels rose at the end of the last **Ice Age**.

Detective work

Use an atlas to find the location of the world's largest islands and coral reefs. Find the islands of Hawaii in the Pacific and the Great Barrier Reef off northeastern Australia. For more information about coral reefs, go to:

weblinks

www.waylinks.co.uk/series/GeogDetective/Coastlines

Coral reefs are made of the shelly remains of sea creatures called coral polyps. The polyps have chalky, cup-shaped skeletons. When the polyps die, their skeletons build up to form reefs. Unusual islands called **coral atolls** are sometimes found in warm, shallow waters off coasts in the **tropics**. These islands are rings of coral which have formed into a circle, often with a **lagoon** in the centre.

Coral reefs are rich in wildlife. The Great Barrier Reef in Australia is home to 3,000 different species, including over 1,000 types of fish.

What is the climate like on the coast?

Climate is the regular pattern of weather in a region. Many coasts have a special **climate**, called a **maritime climate**. Conditions are generally wetter and milder on coasts than in places further inland.

Coasts are often windy places, even when conditions are calm a short way inland.

Coasts are usually wetter than places inland because they lie in the path of wet winds blowing off the ocean. These winds blow in different directions by day and night. By day, warm air rises from the land as it heats up in the sun. Cool air from the sea rushes in to replace the warm air that has risen, cooling the land. This is called an **onshore breeze**. At night the opposite happens: cool air from the land flows towards the sea, creating an **offshore breeze**.

Why do you think the trees shown in the photo are bending over?

DETECTIVE WORK

Next time you are at the beach, look for signs of wild and windy weather on beaches, such as trees growing unevenly and salt damage to huts and boats. During storms, rough seas toss pebbles and debris high on the **shore**.

Palm trees normally grow in hot climates, but these palm trees are growing on Britain's south coast because of the mild climate and warming influence of the Gulf Stream.

The temperature of the sea affects the climate on coastlines. The sea heats up more slowly than the land so that temperatures on coastlines are not too hot in the summer. The sea also loses heat more slowly than the land so that coastal temperatures are not too cold in the winter.

The climate on a coastline is also affected by warm or cool ocean currents. A current is the flow of water in an ocean. Currents are caused by winds and also differences in water temperature in different parts of the oceans. Ocean water generally flows round in giant circles which carry currents close to coastlines.

FOCUS ON

Warm and cool currents

The coasts of western Europe are warmed by a current called the Gulf Stream, which begins in the Gulf of Mexico and flows right across the Atlantic Ocean. Without the Gulf Stream, western Europe would have a much colder climate, similar to that of the island of Newfoundland off Canada. Eastern Canada is cooled by the cold Labrador Current flowing south from the Arctic.

What kinds of wildlife inhabit coasts?

Coasts are rich in wildlife. **Cliffs**, **mudflats**, rocky and sandy **shores** are all home to a different mix of plants and animals. Some coastal species are found nowhere else.

Sea cliffs act as nurseries for birds in spring and summer. Puffins, gannets and gulls lay their eggs on narrow ledges, where they are safe from predators such as foxes. The parent birds catch fish from the ocean and bring it home for the chicks to eat.

These sea lions are resting on a rocky shore in Alaska.

Living things on coasts depend on each other for food. Coastal plants are eaten by small creatures such as worms and shellfish, which in turn are eaten by seabirds.

Rockpools on the beach are home to crabs, shrimps and sea anemones. Limpets and barnacles cling tightly to rocks as the sea crashes over them. Conditions in rockpools change constantly, as tides wash in and out, alternately covering animals with salt water or exposing them to wind and sun.

Sandy beaches can seem barren of life at first. But look closer and you'll find traces of animals such as lugworms that live in underground burrows. Gulls and other shorebirds patrol the water's edge in search of the worms.

Beaches can be divided into four habitats above the waterline: the lower, middle and upper shore and the splash zone. The lower shore is furthest out to sea and is mostly covered by water. Starfish, lobsters and fish called blennies live here. Rockpools on the middle shore are home to sea anemones, dog whelks and mussels. Crabs and barnacles live on the upper shore closest to the shoreline. Sandfleas and sea slaters live higher up, where the sea splashes up at high tide in the salty splash zone.

This rockpool contains many different types of seaweed.

DETECTIVE WORK

Investigate the plants and animals found on your nearest beach. Make a map of the zones on the beach, and draw or photograph the creatures you find in different areas. Don't forget to keep an eye on the tide!

What natural resources are found on coasts?

Modern factory trawlers can net and freeze huge quantities of fish.

Coasts are full of natural resources, including fish and minerals. In recent years people have discovered energy sources, such as oil, in coastal areas.

Since prehistoric times, people have harvested foods such as fish, shellfish and seaweed from **shores** and coastal waters. The first fishermen used hooks, spears and nets to catch their prey. Larger boats and nets, and high-tech equipment now make it easier for modern fishing fleets to catch whole **shoals** of fish.

DETECTIVE WORK

Use the Internet or your local library to find out about natural resources on your nearest coastline. For more information about coastal resources, go to:

weblinks

www.waylinks.co.uk/series/GeogDetective/Coastlines

Oil rigs drill into the seabed to reach pockets of oil and also natural gas, which is often found in the same location.

Energy from the sea

As well as oil and gas, energy from winds, waves and tides can also be used to produce electricity. Tidal power is harnessed in the Bay of Fundy in Canada and on the **estuary** of the River Rance in France. Windmills or wind turbines are seen on many coasts. Wave energy plants are being developed. One day wind may be a major source of power.

Minerals such as tin, copper and nickel are found in coastal waters. Gold and diamonds are collected in a few places where they wash out to sea. Oil and natural gas are mined offshore by oil rigs and processed near the coastline. Sand and gravel are **dredged** (scraped off the bottom) for use in building. However, mining and dredging can harm seabed habitats.

Seawater itself can be useful. Fresh water can be obtained from salt water through a process called **desalination**. Desalination uses a lot of energy, but can be important in regions where there is not much water, such as the Arabian Gulf. Salt is mined from the sea by allowing seawater to flood shallow ponds and then **evaporate** in the sun, leaving the salt behind.

How have people developed coasts?

People settled on coasts in ancient times to harvest food from the sea, and also to use the sea for transporting goods and people. Manufacturing and later tourism became big business. Now, many of the world's largest cities, including New York, Tokyo and Shanghai, are located on coasts.

When ships were invented more than 5,000 years ago, coasts became water highways. For thousands of years, the sea remained a cheap and easy mode of transport. Natural harbours, such as Mumbai in India, offered shelter for ships and grew into busy ports, which became rich through trade.

Mumbai is now a major centre for trade and business. It is one of the world's ten largest cities.

Blue sea, white sand and a warm climate attract tourists to Cancun in Mexico.

Following the Industrial Revolution in the 1700s and 1800s, factories were built around ports that were used to bring raw materials from abroad and also transport finished goods. In factories and power plants, sea water is used for cooling or manufacturing. However, coastal industries can produce pollution (see pages 22–3).

Tourism is now a major source of income in many coastal regions. Around 200 years ago, people began to visit the seaside for holidays and also for their health, to breathe the fresh, salty air. People now flock to coasts around the world to swim, sail, surf, dive or just laze in the sun and enjoy the scenery. Do you have a favourite seaside resort?

Developing paradise

In the last 50 years, cheap air travel has led to the development of tourism in remote places. In the 1970s, developers spotted a beautiful, empty, sandy beach at Cancun, on the coast of Mexico. Cancun is now a major resort, particularly popular with tourists from North America. High-rise hotels with swimming pools line the **shore**.

Are people harming coasts?

Coasts have changed dramatically as ports, resorts and coastal industries have grown. These changes have often had a damaging effect on the natural world.

Coastal waters are the most polluted part of the oceans, because of waste from the land, and also waste dumped at sea.

Where do you think the litter on this beach has come from?

Pollution is now a problem along many coasts. Seas and **shores** are harmed by all sorts of waste, dumped either accidentally or on purpose. Chemicals from factories and farms on coasts and nearby rivers spill into local waters. Towns produce large amounts of sewage, chemicals and also **detergent**, which harm marine life. Waste is dumped or burned by ships in the open ocean. Plastic, metal and glass do not rot, and often wash back onto shore.

DETECTIVE WORK

Carry out a litter survey on a trip to your nearest beach. What types of litter can you see on the shore, and how long do you think it will take for each to rot away? Ask your teacher if you can organise a class trip to clean up litter on the beach.

This bird was caught in oil spilled by the tanker *Prestige* off the coast of Spain, in 2002.

Spilt oil from damaged tankers can cause problems for coasts. In 1989, the wreck of the tanker *Exxon Valdez* off Alaska created a massive oil slick which polluted 1,930 km of coastline. Thousands of birds and sea otters died when their fur or feathers became clogged with oil. In 2002, the oil tanker *Prestige* sank off the coast of Spain, spilling 64,000 tonnes of oil.

Changes brought by humans are affecting the breeding patterns of some marine animals. Seals, seabirds and turtles breed on wild beaches. The growth of resorts, docks and factories means that some of these animals have nowhere to breed. Out to sea, so many fish have been caught that not enough are left to breed. This problem is called over fishing. Seals, whales and dolphins are sometimes caught in fishing nets.

Can coasts be dangerous?

In October 2005, winds battered Miami Beach, Florida, as Hurricane Wilma swept ashore.

Millions of people live on coastlines because of the jobs they are able to do there. However, living on coastlines can be dangerous! Hurricanes, floods, earthquakes and rising sea levels are all threats to coastlines.

Hurricanes are a danger for ships at sea and also coastal settlements. They are huge revolving storms that develop over tropical oceans in warm weather. They can cause great damage when they come ashore. In recent years, several powerful hurricanes have hit the eastern United States. In 1992, Hurricane Andrew caused 25 billion dollars worth of damage in Florida. In August 2005, Hurricane Katrina wrecked towns along the Gulf of Mexico. It also caused the Mississippi River to rise, flooding the city of New Orleans. Some 1,700 people died, and one year later, much of New Orleans had not been rebuilt.

DETECTIVE WORK

Use the Internet or your local library to find out more about the dangers of living in coastal areas. For more about hurricanes and tsunamis, go to:

weblinks

www.waylinks.co.uk/series/GeogDetective/Coastlines

The 2004 Asian tsunami flooded this coastal town in Indonesia. The word tsunami means 'harbour wave' in Japanese.

FOCUS ON

Boxing Day Tsunami 2004

Some of the world's coasts are prone to earthquakes. Undersea earthquakes can cause giant waves called tsunamis. Out to sea these waves are low and hardly noticeable, but they rise up when they reach land. In December 2004, an earthquake off Indonesia caused tsunamis to sweep across the Indian Ocean, swamping coastal towns in Indonesia, Sri Lanka and distant Africa. Up to 300,000 people died.

Sea levels are rising worldwide because the Earth is getting warmer – a problem called **global warming**. This is caused by air pollution as we burn fuels such as oil and coal. Global warming is melting the polar ice caps and making sea levels rise. Rising seas will flood low-lying coasts and may threaten great cities, such as New York, Tokyo and Rotterdam in Holland, may also be affected. Rising sea levels increase the speed of coastal **erosion** (see page 6), while warmer temperatures make storms and hurricanes more likely.

Why do you think tsunamis are called 'harbour waves'?

Rising sea levels threaten low-lying islands, such as the Maldives in the Indian Ocean.

How can people protect coasts?

Coasts have seen many changes in the last century. Pollution and rising sea levels have become a problem, but governments, scientists and ordinary people are now working to protect coastlines. This work is called **conservation**.

FOCUS ON

Preventing erosion

On many coasts, steps are being taken to control **erosion** (see page 6). Sea walls, **dykes** and wooden barriers called **groynes** are built to protect the land from the sea.

This beautiful coastline in Strangford Lough, Northern Ireland is a nature reserve.

Countries around the world are now taking action to clean up pollution. Agreements such as the Law of the Sea Treaty control the dumping of waste on coasts and out to sea. Scientists check for pollution on beaches. The cleanest beaches are given awards, such as the Blue Flag awards in Europe.

By the late twentieth century, **overfishing** had brought some types of fish, such as Newfoundland cod, close to extinction. Whales had also been hunted for centuries, and many species were in danger of dying out. Countries now set limits on the number of fish that can be caught by fishing fleets. The hunting of whales is now generally banned.

Detective work

Find out what conservation groups such as Greenpeace, Friends of the Earth and the World Wide Fund for Nature campaign are doing to conserve our coastlines against pollution and protect coastal wildlife. To find out more information, go to:

weblinks

www.waylinks.co.uk/series/GeogDetective/Coastlines

Many coasts and islands have been made into national parks and reserves. Here, pollution is controlled, and marine life is protected. Coastal reserves protect the breeding beaches of seals, turtles and seabirds. Conservation organisations such as the National Trust in Britain buy wild stretches of coast and carefully control development there. Coral reefs such as the Great Barrier Reef in Australia are now marine parks. In this way, beautiful coastlines and their wildlife will be preserved for years to come.

Whale-watching has become popular, now that whale-hunting is banned.

Your project

If you've done the detective work throughout the book and answered Sherlock's questions, you now know a lot about coastlines! This information will help you to produce your own project about coasts.

First you will need to choose a subject that interests you. You could use one of these questions as a starting point.

Topic questions

- Use your local library and the Internet to find out about life in your nearest port or coastal settlement. How do people earn a living? How have the local **climate** and resources affected the town's development? How has life there changed over the years?
- Compare the way of life in two very different coastal settlements, such as a large port and a small fishing village, or resorts in different parts of the world.
- Use the Internet to find out about a particular coast and its wildlife. How have natural forces helped to shape the coast?

People relax on a beach in Gorey, Jersey with Mont Orguell Castle in the distance.

Your local library and the Internet can provide all sorts of information. You could present your project in an interesting way, perhaps using one of these project presentations.

Sherlock has done a project about coastal mammals such as seals and sea otters. He has learned all about the conservation work that is being done to protect them. Pollution is being reduced so that their habitats are protected and overfishing is being stopped so there is enough food for them to eat.

Project presentation

- Make a map of your chosen coastline in the middle of a large piece of paper. Stick photos or sketches around the map showing local features, wildlife, the coast at high and low tide and in different weather conditions. You could even make a model of the area using clay.

- Imagine you are writing a tourist brochure or making a TV documentary about life in a coastal town or village. Draw a diagram with headings for the major points you want to make and explain all about the region's history.

- Write a story about the coast from the point of view of a fisherman, coastguard or oil rig worker. Write about your life and how it changes during the year.

Coastlines are great places to enjoy lots of different watersports, such as surfing.

Glossary

Bar A spit stretching right across a bay or river mouth.

Barrier island A type of island made of sandy materials dropped offshore where coastal currents are weak.

Circulate To move around in a circle.

Cliff A steep rock wall at the coast.

Climate The long-term weather pattern of a region.

Conservation Work done in order to protect nature.

Coral atoll An island made of coral, often in the form of a ring surrounding a lagoon.

Desalination To remove salt from something.

Detergent Soap and other cleaning products.

Dredge To scrape off the bottom.

Dyke A bank built to prevent flooding or keep back the sea.

Erosion The gradual wearing away of the land by wind, water or ice.

Estuary The mouth or lower stretch of a river, regularly washed by salt water from the sea.

Evaporate To change from a liquid to a gas.

Fjord A steep-sided inlet formed when ice eroded the land in coastal areas, and was later flooded by the sea.

Global warming A general rise in world temperatures, caused by a build-up of gases in the air which trap the Sun's heat.

Gravity The pull of the Earth, Moon or Sun on an object.

Groyne A wooden barrier on a beach which helps to prevent erosion.

Ice Ages Long, cold periods in Earth's history, during which ice covered more of the land than it does today.

Lava Hot, melted rock erupted by volcanoes.

Lagoon A coastal lake which is separated from the sea by rocks or a spit.

Longshore drift The sideways movement of sand or pebbles along the coast, due to waves striking the shore at an angle.

Maritime climate The regular pattern of weather on the coast.

Mudflat A flattish bank of mud, often found near the mouth of a river.

Roller A low wave in the open ocean.

Offshore breeze A wind blowing from the land towards the sea.

Onshore breeze A wind blowing from the sea towards the land.

Overfishing When fishermen catch so many fish that few are left to breed, so that the fish population gets smaller.

Saltmarsh A boggy area found near the coast and regularly washed by the tides.

Shingle Pebbles or gravel that cover some beaches.

Shoal A large group of fish.

Shore The land bordering a sea or a lake.

Spit A long, narrow finger of land stretching out into the sea or a river.

Stack A natural pillar of rock standing out to sea.

Tidal range The difference in height between sea levels at high and low tide.

Tropics Areas around the equator (the invisible line round the middle of the Earth, which is the same distance from the North and South Poles).

Answers

Page 7 The sea carries seaweed, driftwood and other debris to the back of the beach, forming a line called the high tide mark.

Page 14 Trees growing on coasts are often bent by powerful winds blowing off the ocean, called onshore breezes.

Page 22 Crates and debris from fishing boats may have washed in from ports or boats at sea. Some of the rubbish may have been carried out to sea by rivers and then washed back onto the coastline.

Page 25 Tsunamis are called 'harbour waves' because they form quite low waves out to sea, and only rise up when they reach the shallow waters of harbours and coasts.

Further Information

Books to read

Saving Oceans and Wetlands by Jen Green, Chrysalis Books, 2004

Earth's Changing Coasts by Neil Morris, Raintree, 2003

Coasts by Louise and Richard Spilsbury, Heinemann Library, 2004

Bustling Coastline, by Barbara Taylor, Ticktock Media, 2000

The Mud Pack: Sea and Shore by James Parry, National Trust, 2002

Earth in Danger: Coasts by Polly Goodman, Wayland 2005

Coasts of the British Isles by Terry Jennings, Evans Brothers, 2001

The Geography Detective Investigates: Seaside Towns by Nicola Barber, Wayland 2007

Websites:

The National Trust:
www.nationaltrust.org.uk/coastline

Check this site for more information on coasts:
http://coastline.nationaltrust.org.
uk/kids/index

Environmental Investigation Agency:
www.eia-international.org
World Conservation Monitoring Centre:
www.wcmc.org.uk

Marine Conservation Society: www.mcsuk.org

Index

The Geography Detective Investigates

Contents of all books in the series:

Your Local Area 978 07502 4817 4
Where are you?
How would you describe the landscape around you?
What's the story behind where you live?
How has the population changed over time?
What do people do where you live?
How accessible is your local area?
Where does the food you eat come from?
What's the weather like where you live?
Where does all the water come from?
What else lives in your local area?
How environmentally sustainable is your local area?
How can you look after your local area?
Your project

Rivers 978 07502 4816 7
What are rivers?
How do rivers begin?
How do rivers shape the landscape?
Why don't rivers run straight?
What happens as rivers approach the sea?
What kinds of wildlife inhabit rivers?
Why do people depend on rivers?
How do we put rivers to work?
How are rivers good for transportation?
Why do towns develop near rivers?
Are people harming rivers?
How can we take care of rivers?
Your project

Mountains 978 07502 5048 1
What are mountains?
How do mountains form?
How are mountains shaped?
What is mountain weather like?
What plants grow on mountains?
How do animals live on mountains?
How do we use mountains?
How do people live in mountain areas?
What work do people do?
Why is travel difficult in mountain areas?
Are mountains dangerous?
How can we take care of mountains?
Your project

Villages 978 07502 5050 4
What is a village?
How are villages laid out?
What types of houses are there?
What landmarks can you find in villages?
What are village schools like?
What services are there?
What jobs do people do?
What traditions do villagers celebrate?
What plants and animals live in villages?
How do villages change?
What is Wharram Percy?
What is the future for villages?
Your project

Coastlines 978 07502 5049 8
What are coastlines?
What forces shape coastlines?
How are coastlines shaped by erosion?
How do beaches, spits and bars form?
How do islands and coral reefs form?
What is the climate like on the coast?
What kinds of wildlife inhabit coasts?
What natural resources are found on coasts?
How have people developed coasts?
Are people harming coasts?
Can coasts be dangerous?
How can we protect coasts?
Your project

Seaside Towns 978 07502 5051 1
What are seaside towns?
How did seaside towns start?
What are piers, causeways and breakwaters?
Who lives in seaside towns?
What kind of buildings do you find in seaside towns?
What do people do in seaside towns?
How do people travel to seaside towns?
Why do people visit seaside towns?
What wildlife can you spot at the seaside?
How have people affected the seaside environment?
What are the hazards of living in seaside towns?
How do seaside towns protect themselves from the sea?
Your project

WAYLAND